Joseph

The power of forgiveness and reconciliation

Elizabeth Rundle

Published 2003 by CWR, Waverley Abbey House, Waverley Lane,
Farnham, Surrey GU9 8EP, UK. Registered Charity No. 294387. Registered
Limited Company No. 1990308.
Reprinted 2007.

See back of book for list of National Distributors.

Concept development, editing, design and production by CWR.
Front cover image: Roger Walker.
Printed in England by IQ Laserpress.

ISBN: 978-1-85345-252-9

Contents

Introduction		1
Week 1	Teenager with Attitude	5
Week 2	Sold into Egypt	11
Week 3	Dreams	17
Week 4	A Man of Distinction	23
Week 5	Corn in Egypt	29
Week 6	Forgiveness and Reconciliation	35
Week 7	Conclusion	41
Leader's Notes		47

Introduction

With 13 chapters in Genesis devoted to the unfolding story of Joseph, we seem to know more about his life than that of practically any other person in the Old Testament. We meet Joseph as a 17-year-old lad and follow the twists and turns of his fortunes until his death at 'one hundred and ten'.

Although the life of Joseph stands on its own as a fascinating family drama, the author's overriding reason for making so much of the story was purely theological. Whereas most people immediately think of Joseph's colourful coat, the great theme to concern biblical writers was God's providential care. Throughout Joseph's life, in the darkest situations, God turned the evil of man's intentions and activities into a catalyst for good.

There was another fundamental reason for this story. In the time of Jacob, the covenant promise made by God to Abraham and his descendants seemed far from being realised. As we read these chapters, we can see how easily the Israelites could have been wiped out by the great famine. However, Joseph, Abraham's great-grandson, becomes their saviour and, rather than being starved into oblivion, the story shows how the Israelites came to live and prosper in Egypt. It is also clear that Joseph himself, at the end of his life, looked forward confidently to the fulfilment of God's promise. He knew that his God had been ever present and would be faithful to His promise.

Such is the skill of the storyteller that by the end we feel we know Joseph and the rest of the cast. The family tensions and temptations leap from the pages of Genesis in a startlingly contemporary fashion. Joseph's unconditional faith and perseverance through the vicissitudes of life draws out our admiration for the man, and he comes across as one of the genuinely decent and honourable characters in the Old Testament.

Joseph was one of 12 sons born to Jacob from four women – Leah, Rachel, Leah's servant girl, Zilpah, and Rachel's servant girl, Bilhah. We know from chapter 34 that there was at least one daughter, Dinah, but in the patriarchal society it was only the sons who counted. Rachel was Jacob's favourite wife and Joseph became the favourite son. Tragically, on the way to Bethlehem, Rachel died giving birth to Benjamin (chap. 35) and to this day Rachel's tomb, on the road just outside Bethlehem, is still venerated as a holy place for Jews.

It is interesting to note Jacob's 12 sons, because so much is made of 'the twelve tribes of Israel', yet Joseph did not give his name to a 'tribe'. The line passed to Joseph's sons, Manasseh and Ephraim (Josh. 16:4ff.). This is somewhat an enigma, because Joseph was such a great hero, even the Egyptian Pharaoh recognised his deep spirituality (Gen. 41:38).

It is not necessary to have precise dates for the validity of the Joseph story. Historians and archaeologists plough through complex data to make sense of the jigsaw which was the Near East in second millennium BC when nomadic groups wandered along trade routes. Somewhere between 1880 and 1680 BC appears to be the most probable date, and chapter 47 tells us how Jacob, all the family, flocks and herds, settled in Goshen after rediscovering Joseph and fleeing from the famine in Israel. This was an area round the fertile north-eastern part of Egypt where irrigation guaranteed the crops. After this period the Pharaohs based their capital further south.

Clearly, Jacob and the rest of the family received a friendly welcome into Egypt – what a contrast for their descendants! However, they remained a separate group from the main population as Egyptian culture was felt to be superior to shepherds and nomads. So, the background to this story is a picture of Egypt as a reliable ally to surrounding nations in time of famine, international trade caravans passing through Syria, Canaan, down the Nile Delta and beyond. There appeared to be relative freedom of movement before the spread of nationalism began the rise of great empires.

This inspired Word of God originated as oral tradition, passed from generation to generation before the actual written account became revered Scripture. It is awesome to realise that these chapters deal with issues and tensions which confront people today, jealousy, infidelity, fear, betrayal and hunger.

Although we know that Rachel died in childbirth, we do not know how old Joseph was at the time. Modern psychologists could offer fascinating insights into how the young Joseph might have been affected by the death of his mother, which may have triggered his irritating boasting. But whatever the story does not tell us, it nevertheless manages to lift the curtain on the life of the extended family of those times, the nature of work, agriculture, travel and world politics. It is an intensely human story permeated with divine presence. Through mystery and miracle, we acknowledge that the God whom Joseph worshipped is the same unchanging God who is able to direct His purposes through modern lives to speak to our world with beacons of justice, truth, honour, compassion, reconciliation and forgiveness.

Enjoy this beautifully crafted story and let the Lord God guide your life.

WEEK 1

Teenager with Attitude

Opening Icebreaker

Go around the group introducing yourselves by name if you don't know each other and say which colour or colour combination you enjoy wearing and which you feel best suits your personality.

Bible Readings

- Genesis 37
- Leviticus 27:1–7
- 1 Samuel 17:17–29
- Luke 22:4–5

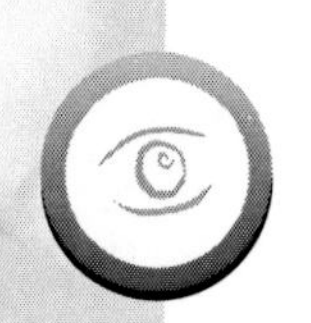

Opening Our Eyes

This chapter is a powder keg of raw emotions and their consequences.

Anyone with stepbrothers and sisters will be only too familiar with the adolescent bickering implied at the start of this chapter. Joseph was the favourite son of Jacob's favourite wife, Rachel, who had died when Joseph was a little boy (Gen. 35:16–20). Joseph used adolescent skill in playing this favouritism to his advantage. You might also consider what his brothers may have been doing behind their father's back which prompted Joseph to inform on them.

It is ironic that Jacob was Rebekah's favourite son, a situation which led to the deception of Isaac and the older brother, Esau, yet Jacob repeated this unhelpful pattern with Joseph. He makes matters worse by indulging the boy with the present of that flashy coat. This may not have been exactly 'a technicolour dream-coat', more a specially-patterned, long-sleeved coat, a completely unsuitable garment and glaringly different from the plain tunics of working shepherds. It was like giving Joseph rank and privilege over his brothers, removing him from the responsibilities and hard work expected from the rest of the household. But before we judge, how often have we witnessed children being compensated by parents for some loss in their young lives?

When Joseph told his brothers about his dreams (and we shall be looking in greater detail at the content of these dreams in Week 3), we can imagine they were only too pleased to disappear with the flocks and get far away from their unbearably self-important brother. The route they took would have covered some 50 miles and offers a glimpse into the life of nomadic shepherds of Canaan.

What happened next indicates that the story may have been pieced together by ancient editors from two different sources, as both Midianites and Ishmaelites are mentioned within the same verse (v.28). Dothan was on the major trade route to and from Egypt, and caravans would be continuously passing along this biblical M25. Take a quick peek forward to chapter 42 verse 21. It rounds off the picture of the boy's terror. Sold to slave-traders, Joseph, like all slaves of the time, would have walked into Egypt naked and shackled.

The chapter ends with Jacob inconsolable. Himself a wily conman, Jacob was most cruelly deceived by those he trusted most. Meanwhile, Joseph, bruised and humiliated, was dragged off into a foreign country to be sold like an animal.

Discussion Starters

1. Is there a member of the group who grew up feeling another sibling was 'the favourite'? It could be helpful to discuss this.

2. Is there anyone who realises they had preferential treatment which caused bad feeling between siblings?

3. This ancient account predates Moses and the Ten Commandments, yet the brothers automatically knew that it was evil to murder their brother. Exchange ideas about 'instinctive morality'. How much might these basic instincts be motivated by belief in a God?

4. Imagine you are part of a trading caravan. What difficulties would you expect to encounter on your long journeys and compare some of those difficulties with today's international traders?

5. Leviticus 27:1–7 lays down the price for slaves of different age and gender in a most matter of fact way. The buying and selling of children and adults is still taking place today. What kind of situations force families into slavery now?

6. Presumably the brothers loved their father. Consider how much Jacob had made his sons hate Joseph that they were able to live with the deception that must have broken Jacob's heart.

7. Thousands of people are reported 'missing' each year. How is it so easy to completely disappear? Pray for any current missing people on the news or within your locality.

8. Jealousy is one of the 'deadly sins'. Talk together about the misunderstandings and divisions caused in families and churches by jealousy and offer ideas to overcome this emotion.

Personal Application

In this opening chapter of the Joseph story we are faced with common situations and deep emotions. But we also see how God enables us to find purpose and positive outcome in the bleakest of circumstances.

Have you been a motherless teenager or perhaps an overcompensating single parent? Have you felt jealous of a brother or sister or have you deceived somebody you loved? Have you known about something which was wrong but never spoken out?

These subjects touch us at our most personal level and can be painful to face. Even if you have never had any of these experiences, the Scripture narratives are enormously helpful in our understanding of others. Joseph could do nothing about his situation except trust the God of his father and grandfather. We too can trust God.

Seeing Jesus in the Scriptures

There are just amazing parallels between the lives of Joseph and our Lord Jesus.

The chief priests and the rulers of the Temple were jealous and connived to get rid of Jesus (Luke 19:47), and Judas sold his Lord as Joseph was also sold (Luke 22:4–5). Jesus suffered humiliation when His robe was taken from Him (John 19:23–24). Joseph too had his status ripped away when the brothers took his coat. Joseph's life dramatises one of the great biblical themes, that of a suffering servant, the one who suffers abuse and scorn who will be lifted up by God for the salvation of others.

WEEK 2

Sold into Egypt

Opening Icebreaker

Tell each other who or what you have left at home as you meet with the group.

Bible Readings

- Genesis 39
- Psalm 139:7–12
- Hebrews 4:15

Opening Our Eyes

So Joseph, minus his coat of many colours, arrived in Egypt. It would have been a long, arduous journey for a lad shielded even from the normal family chores with the stock. It is fair to imagine he had lost weight and that his bare feet would have been in a mess from blisters and cuts from the rough road. Then journey's end was the horror of the human marketplace.

However awful Joseph was feeling, he evidently looked a decent specimen of slave to Potiphar, Captain of Pharaoh's Guard. Joseph found himself in quite a good position, living, probably for the first time in his life, in a house. Archaeologists tell us that the houses of rich and influential people were often three-storeyed with balconies, furnished with rugs and hand-carved chairs. Quite a culture shock for a boy who would have been used to sitting by the tent gazing at the stars.

Within this chapter there are four references to the Lord being with Joseph. He might have been idle and spoiled by his father but nonetheless Jacob had instilled into his son fear of the Lord God and a high moral code. This is all the more interesting in the light of the early life of his father and also the exploits of his brother Judah (chap. 38).

Joseph was such a reliable and pleasing slave that, over time, he rose to be the equivalent of an estate manager. In verse 6 we see a reference to the food taboos of Egypt long before the rigid food laws adopted in Moses' time.

Literature, ancient or modern, sooner or later gets down to themes of sexual temptation and the consequences. The Bible is no exception and contains many such stories. However, in the episode with Potiphar's wife, the handsome young Joseph seems to become a victim all over again. This Egyptian lady, with time on her hands, made a determined effort to seduce the attractive foreign slave; so much so the writer states that she spoke to him 'day after day' (v.10).

When she finally cornered Joseph, his loyalty to his master and his own high principles left him no alternative but to run from the house. We then witness the about turn from velvet seductress to furious spurned woman. In her spite and humiliation she lies through her teeth and waits for Potiphar to act. The fact that Potiphar didn't have Joseph instantly killed may indicate a genuine fondness for the young man and even a slight uncertainty as to where the exact truth lay.

Joseph's world had collapsed once more. Prison! Prison was the place for guilty people and there was little effort to bring criminals to trial. Therefore, a foreign slave had no chance of justice. Yet even here in this predicament, the Lord was with Joseph. It wasn't the ordinary prison into which Joseph had been thrown but the one where the king's prisoners were kept – a special category of prison.

The jailor recognised him as trustworthy and reliable so that, as second-in-command of the jail, life became a little more tolerable. But the Lord God had a greater purpose in store for Jacob's favourite son than being a prison warder ...

Discussion Starters

1. In what ways do you think Potiphar would have recognised the Lord was with Joseph?

2. It could be argued that sexual temptation is the strongest temptation of all. Discuss this story line in relation to current television 'soaps'.

3. What qualities did Joseph show in resisting Potiphar's wife?

4. Why do you think Joseph was put into prison rather than executed?

5. What other kind of people could be in this special category of prison?

6. Joseph never seemed to whinge or be revengeful, nor did he lose his faith even in dreadful situations beyond his control. How have you reacted when wrongly accused of something?

7. Joseph's misfortunes seemed to enrich his faith. How do you think that these times strengthened his character?

8. Joseph stood apart as a young man of integrity. How would you recognise faith and integrity in a foreigner today? Then think of people you have noticed who stand out from the crowd. Are they people of faith?

9. Recognising the presence of God in our lives should automatically lift our moral standards, so all Christians should be 'different'. Discuss the difference between churchgoing and Christianity.

Personal Application

When bad things happen to us, it is so easy to sulk, complain and blame everybody including God. From Joseph we see that it is possible to face situations with God's strength and to bring about some glimmer of goodness from a seemingly hopeless and devastating experience. We have much to learn from him about perseverance, optimism and straightforward decency.

Joseph behaved with the same integrity in prison as within Potiphar's house. It is a rare gift to behave the same way wherever we are for there are so many things which can throw us off spiritual balance.

From Joseph's experience we can be inspired to pray for God's presence and strength in all things and trust Him to work out His purpose despite human manipulation. He challenges us to worship the Lord by the way we live, for we are ambassadors for Christ wherever we are – and we are never alone.

Seeing Jesus in the Scriptures

The recurring theme in the Old Testament of the suffering servant, the victim who fearlessly keeps faith, culminates in the life of our Lord Jesus who, as the victim on the cross, conquers death to offer salvation to all believers. The repetition of 'the LORD was with him' also has resonance for when Jesus, in the synagogue at Nazareth, proclaimed Isaiah's words: 'The Spirit of the Lord is on me' (Luke 4:18). Joseph was tempted, arrested for a crime he had not committed and thrown into prison. Jesus was 'tempted in every way, just as we are – yet was without sin' (Heb. 4:15) and was arrested, beaten and humiliated.

WEEK 3

Dreams

Opening Icebreaker

Experts tell us that everyone dreams, even though not many of our dreams are recalled in the light of day. Have any of you had a dream which has stayed in your mind, or, if you do not wish to volunteer a dream, you could briefly describe your dream occupation!

Bible Readings

- Genesis 37:5–11; 40:1–41:32
- Deuteronomy 13:1–5
- Joel 2:28–32

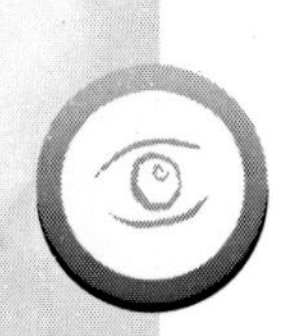

Opening Our Eyes

Martin Luther King's speech, 'I have a dream ...' may rank as one of the most influential speeches of the twentieth century. An entirely different sort of dream from dreams which remain in our minds in vivid fragments but for which we have no explanation. In the Joseph story we look at six important dreams.

Let's remember that the setting of this story is about Middle Bronze Age and each society had its own attitude to dreams. It's interesting to see how the Israelite attitude to dreams changes significantly according to time and place. Most Near East countries adopted the view that dreams were prophetic and the Egyptians developed the interpretation of dreams into a highly specialised art. The patriarchs also accepted that their God revealed Himself in dreams (Gen. 20:3; 31:24; Num. 12:6). Much further on in their history, after Moses had led the people out of Egypt, there was obviously a frosty attitude to dreams (Deut. 13:1–5). But then again, it all becomes acceptable in the Nativity accounts (see Matt. 1:20 and 2:19).

However, back to Joseph. Clearly, like a modern teenager, Joseph saw himself as the centre of the universe and he pompously – and most unwisely – described his dreams to his family. His brothers would have taken this to imply that Joseph saw himself as divinely favoured which was hardly likely to be an endearing trait and only fuelled their anger and resentment.

The fact that Joseph compounds his alienation by bragging of the second dream makes the point that a duplicated 'message' carried great significance.

When it comes to the dreams of Pharaoh's cup-bearer and baker, we have an insight into the heart and mind of the mature Joseph. In a key verse (40:8), we realise the depth of Joseph's faith in his acknowledgement of his God. To an Egyptian this would have been a colossal snub from an insignificant semi-nomad from the land of Canaan. However, these previously influential men were prepared to listen to the young Hebrew. But look at the thanks he got! The cup-bearer may have had good intentions but he proved unreliable. Surely Joseph had good reason to feel despondent.

Joseph languishes for two years before the next dreams, when Pharaoh became so disturbed by his nightmares that he called for the most revered magicians and occult practitioners in his kingdom.

When Joseph was summoned, the picture is painted of a quiet young man who combined a serene dignity with genuine humility. Before Pharaoh he placed all the emphasis on his God to interpret the puzzling dreams. The writer of this story is saying that interpretation of dreams is no man-made art or science but the work of God; also that warnings of disaster, like those of the prophets to come, could be countered by new directions. This young man from Canaan offered simple words of wisdom to the sophisticated Egyptian king.

Discussion Starters

1. Joseph had had the best of clothes, the over-indulgence of his father and an inflated opinion of himself. What modern correlation could be put on this not-so-happy-family picture?

2. Consider the difficulties for Joseph in maintaining his faith in his father's God. Compare his situation with that of Daniel (Dan. 6:10).

3. How would you maintain your faith in hostile surroundings?

4. Imagine the reaction of Pharaoh's cup-bearer if the baker had been first to have his dream interpreted.

5. Think about the current situation in the world where people are imprisoned without trial. What sustains them?

6. Thinking of the challenging words of Jesus in Matthew 25:36ff., how do you view your Christian response to prison and prisoners in general?

7. Joseph automatically gave God the glory rather than himself. What revelations or marvellous discoveries do you automatically identify with and give glory to individuals?

8. Look closely at Genesis 41:38. Discuss the personal traits that Pharaoh saw in Joseph and which marked him out as a believer of a different God? Do people see us as different?

Personal Application

The prophet Joel said that those who faithfully called on the Lord would be saved. Faith was Joseph's lifeline. Is it yours? When our dreams don't come true, Satan cunningly beguiles us into doubts and cynicism. It can be tempting to turn to all the available clairvoyants, card-readers and crystal gazers – but the lesson of Joseph is that only God is the interpreter of dreams. We need to forge a closer walk with our Lord so that prayerfully we may discern the right way forward in our lives. The world needs people with vision and dreams and the faith to see how life should be: a world of shared resources, of justice and freedom and the peace of God in all our relationships – personal, national and international.

Seeing Jesus in the Scriptures

In his integrity and dignity, Joseph was a forerunner of our Lord Jesus. Joseph was falsely accused and put in prison. When Jesus was arrested and imprisoned without a proper trial, He took all the false accusations, scourging and humiliation without fighting back. As Joseph had given time and compassion to the butler and the baker, so Jesus had time and compassion, even at the point of His greatest suffering, to comfort the men crucified with Him. We associate Psalm 22 with Jesus feeling forsaken by His Father but, if you read it all the way through, you will find verses of fantastic faith: 'For he has not despised or disdained the suffering of the afflicted one ... but has listened to his cry for help.'

From the cross Jesus offered a vision of eternity with Him – paradise.

WEEK 4

A Man of Distinction

Opening Icebreaker

Make a list of all the 'gods' the group can think of, eg Greek gods, Norse gods and so on, then make another list of different faiths today.

Bible Readings

- Genesis 41:33–57
- Psalm 105:16–22
- Philippians 3:13–14

Opening Our Eyes

We have moved on some 13 years since Joseph last saw his family. This is an intriguing chapter as it blends archaeology, geography, culture and economics with the personal fortunes of our central character. We need always to remember that this story was a lovingly recited oral tradition long before it became written literature, but it is no surprise that its authenticity is confirmed by non-biblical sources from the time.

Psalm 105 graphically portrays Joseph's plight before he became the 'trusty' in the prison. The interesting division between the Semitic and Egyptian cultures comes into focus in the picture of the released Joseph immediately having to shave and change his clothes. Egyptians did not grow beards and they favoured white linen clothes. We take it as implied that after so long in the dungeon he also washed! An inscribed cylinder, found in 1878, Rassam Cylinder, documents the investiture of a vice-regent: 'I clad him in a garment with multicoloured trimmings, placed a gold chain on him ... put golden rings on his hands. I presented him with chariots, mules and horses.' Therefore we can be certain that Joseph's investiture bears authentic features.

When we look at the geography of both Canaan and Egypt, it is obvious how the River Nile was the life-blood of Egypt; the annual flooding brought rich silt to the land and it was the source of irrigation. The Egyptians used this to great advantage, while the land of Canaan was totally dependent upon rainfall for its water supply. The governmental structures of ancient Egypt were such that Joseph's ideas for storing grain would have been the perfect solution, and vast granaries are actually mentioned in Egyptian records.

Joseph had now risen as high as any non-royal could. He is called Zaphenath-Paneah and has become, to all intents and purposes, an Egyptian citizen. To reinforce his status, Pharaoh arranged a marriage to Asenath, daughter of a priest who worshipped the sun-god, Ra.

This then was a makeover the like of which had never been known before. The favourite son was back in favour and all of Egypt honoured him. One might think that with his newly acquired fame and fortune, Joseph would have closed the past from his mind. But, on the birth of his sons, he gave them names from Canaan. Manasseh, meaning 'God has made me forget' and Ephraim, 'God has made me fruitful'.

Against all the odds Joseph did not turn his back on the God of his father, Jacob. He could not ignore the blood ties and the inextricable link between tribe and deity; he had a deep and unashamed faith in his God, even though surrounded by Egypt's gods. Here was a man of true integrity. Three times in chapter 41 Joseph directs all praise from himself and points to the authority of God, both in revealing His message and in empowering the people to live through their crisis.

The predominant message here is that those who are open to the voice of God and who are prepared to be faithful to His Word, will receive blessing and bring blessing to their situation. Joseph was a channel of God's blessing, first to a people who followed other gods and then to his own people. The Bible once again challenges us by the inclusiveness of God's providence.

Discussion Starters

1. The world is a vastly different place today from the time of the Pharaohs and yet some religions are still identifiable by their adherents' dress. Consider the clothing differences between Buddhist monks and ultra-Orthodox Jews. What are the theological reasons for being set apart?

2. What lessons can we learn from Joseph's agricultural policy which could be making a difference to famine situations today?

3. Joseph and Asenath came from totally different backgrounds and worshipped different gods. Discuss the positive and negative aspects of such a marriage.

4. 'Look to the rock from which you were cut and to the quarry from which you were hewn' (Isa. 51:1). How does our 'beginning' shape the rest of our life?

5. It may be interesting for members of the group to disclose which person in their lives has most influenced their faith.

6. What kind of stories do you suppose Joseph would have told to Manasseh and Ephraim when he returned from overseeing storehouses in various parts of Egypt?

7. Would there be ways in which not being Egyptian might have made Joseph's responsibility for grain storage and distribution easier?

8. Imagine Joseph's life in Egypt, the robes, the adornments of office, the chariots, the house, servants, new family ...

9. Joseph was 30 when charged with the task of saving the nation from famine. Contrast his life with the life of Jesus who began His saving ministry at 30 years of age.

Personal Application

We find it so difficult to let go of past wrongs and make a new start. Joseph is a shining example of how people should get on with their lives. He 'forgot' his past in the sense that he was not consumed by bitterness, hatred, the eternal 'if only' and self-pitying 'why me?'. We see in Joseph's demeanour the triumph of integrity, courage, wisdom and a total reliance upon God. It is such a temptation for us to be self-seeking and look for rewards, to make a great noise about our rights with scant regard for our responsibilities. If we consider that our God can be honoured by the way we live and publicly relate to our faith, it should make a whole new difference to the way we conduct ourselves. Look at Philippians 3:13–14.

Seeing Jesus in the Scriptures

Pharaoh saw the Spirit of God in Joseph and immediately we recognise the importance of this phrase. Luke 3:22 records the Holy Spirit descending on Jesus at His baptism; in the synagogue in Nazareth, Jesus read from the scroll of Isaiah 61 reiterating the words 'The Spirit of the Lord is on me...' and even the centurion at the foot of the cross was moved to acknowledge Jesus was the Son of God (Matt. 27:54).

All the great names of Old Testament history become overshadowed by Jesus, the Name above all names. What others struggled to be and do, our Lord Jesus perfected in Himself. He saves us from the materialism and emptiness of secular life with the bread of eternal life.

WEEK 5

Corn in Egypt

Opening Icebreaker

If you were snowed-in for several weeks, what would each of you want to have in your store cupboard? Would you exchange in order to help your neighbour, and with which commodities?

Bible Readings

- Genesis 42:1–43:14; 43:24–44:33

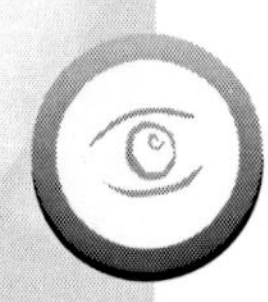

Opening Our Eyes

This is one of the most detailed and gripping episodes in the Old Testament with all the hallmarks of high drama and suspense. The severe famine, which God had forewarned, had taken hold of 'all the world' (41:57), as well as Egypt. The prudent agrarian strategy of Zaphenath-Paneah was paying dividends.

In this deceptively simple narrative, we trace how the people of Israel got themselves down to Egypt in the first place, as well as listening in to the guilt and recriminations amongst the ten brothers and the overwhelming grief of the old father. Although the characters come alive with the storyteller's consummate skill, it is clear, as it has been from the beginning, that God, Yahweh, El Shaddai, was ever present, ever guiding and bringing redemption out of disaster.

Can we blame Joseph for his games of cat and mouse? Is he trying to find out whether his brothers are the same unpleasant bunch he remembers from his youth, or is this a darker side of Joseph? To accuse them of spying was quite realistic as records show that several fortifications were built along the Egyptian border to resist incursions from the north. Spying, after all, goes on in every culture.

Joseph understands their whispered despair (42:21). It is a stark reminder of the brothers' callousness all those years before and therefore it is a gesture of immense grace when Joseph, who had been sold for money, orders that each man should have his money for the grain secretly returned.

Poor old Jacob appears suffocatingly over-protective of Benjamin. He is so desperate to cling to his youngest son, the son of his old age with his favourite wife, Rachel, that the strapping adult he must have been by then is spoken of as a child. However, when Jacob realises that Benjamin has to return with the brothers for a further supply of grain – not first and foremost the release of Simeon! – then it's interesting to note the gifts he tells them to take to 'the man' in Egypt (43:11).

The banquet Joseph ordered for the brothers kept to the cultural etiquette of the time when Egyptians felt themselves too refined and cultivated to eat with vulgar herdsmen from neighbouring lands. The brothers squirmed with guilt, apprehension and embarrassment. As readers, we obviously recall Joseph's youthful dreams of his brothers' obeisance; those dreams would have been disregarded years before by the brothers, but his father would not have forgotten (37:11).

As the story unfolds towards its climax, a neat little ruse throws the brothers into further panic. This time Judah, the brother who had suggested Joseph be sold rather than killed, gives one of the most eloquent speeches of the Old Testament. From this outpouring of concern for his father and his self-sacrificial offer to lose his own liberty, Joseph knew in his heart that his brothers had changed. He could not wait any longer to heal the family rift.

Discussion Starters

1. In our land of plenty, it is difficult for us to imagine a famine, but how would you feel about going to another country to beg for food for your family?

2. How do we, as a relatively rich country, or as individuals, respond to those who are blighted by famine in their lands and when we have appeals from various charities?

3. How important to you is trust with family and close friends? If that trust is completely destroyed, how do you seek (or is it possible) to mend the relationship?

4. Do you consider Joseph was being fair or vengeful as he tested his brothers?

5. How do you think Jacob felt when he realised his sons had deceived him for over 20 years?

6. Put yourself in Simeon's shoes and imagine what your feelings would be to see your brothers go back home without you.

7. Looking at 43:9 do you feel that Judah has changed and what might have brought about that change?

8. Considering the family was in the grip of such severe famine it is touching that Jacob should arrange a bag of gifts for the viceroy. Does anyone in the group have experience to share of peoples' generosity from great poverty?

Personal Application

Families can cause the greatest joy and the greatest heartache. Each family is different but, as we look at Jacob's, we see how the ripples of hurt affect family members over long periods of time. Maybe there is a situation in your family where relationships have been broken and resentment has smouldered on unchecked. This family saga from ancient memory portrays Joseph as a man who didn't allow his life to be eaten up with bitterness. He trusted God's far-reaching purposes and was willing to show mercy and compassion. It's comparatively easy to feel hard done by and the victim, but far more difficult to acknowledge that we may have been the means of somebody else's anguish. If there is a situation where you have the opportunity to build bridges, think how Joseph acted – and also think what Jesus would do.

Seeing Jesus in the Scriptures

Judah is the first person in the Bible to show a willingness to sacrifice himself for the sake of another. This great theme of self-sacrifice appears again in the writings of Isaiah in the concept of the suffering servant and finds its culmination in the death of our Lord Jesus Christ. Also, by the way in which Joseph was able to save his family and therefore continue the covenant promise which had been given to Abraham, so Jesus spoke of His death as being: 'the new covenant in my blood' (1 Cor. 11:25). Joseph saved his people with grain; Jesus saves His people with spiritual food, for He is the bread of life (John 6:35).

WEEK 6

Forgiveness and Reconciliation

Opening Icebreaker

Imagine you have to uproot *all* your family, pets and/or livestock, and move to another country to live and work. Which country would you choose for a new home and why? Would you have 'trouble' with any member of the family over such a move?

Bible Readings

- Genesis 45:1–46:7, 28–30; 47:5–12
- 2 Corinthians 5:17–21
- Hebrews 7:7

Opening Our Eyes

The emotional atmosphere is electric as Joseph weeps uncontrollably – at last he has reconnected to his family roots. How often over those intervening years must he have longed to see his father and his brothers again, especially Benjamin, and now he is able to embrace his brothers and bid them to hurry back to bring Jacob down into Egypt.

Touching though this family reunion is, it is immediately clear that Joseph has an important point to make. He reassures his brothers that he harbours no grudges against them because whatever their evil intentions had been all those years before, their actions have been overridden by God's providence. Notice how Joseph stresses four times that God had sent him to Egypt, not that the brothers were trying to get rid of him, but that God's purposes to preserve life were ultimately fulfilled.

This says much about Joseph's faith and also about the writer's motive in making sure the readers acknowledge God's faithfulness to His covenant with Abraham to be a great nation and a blessing to all peoples (Gen. 12:2–3). These fascinating biographical glimpses are in actual fact totally God-centred. They were passed on from generation to generation to show how throughout the history of Abraham's descendants, the one true God of Israel used individuals, often under great stress, as channels of His love and mercy to bring about His divine purposes (see Rom. 9:16–17).

What a magnanimous gesture on Joseph's part to send his brothers home loaded with provisions and gifts. With all the Egyptian power at his disposal, he could have retaliated against the brothers with vindictive spite, but no, he forgave and showered good things on those who had robbed him of everything. This is true forgiveness.

Notice how Joseph, the boy who had swanned about in the multi-coloured coat, now lavishes five sets of clothes on his beloved younger brother, Benjamin.

How was Jacob going to react to his favourite son being found alive? And not only alive but in such an exalted position. Jacob was by this time extremely elderly and, like many people as they grow older, he seemed preoccupied with his own imminent demise. He was understandably reticent about trudging off down to Egypt because in his memory would have been the famine that enticed his grandfather Abraham into Egypt – with somewhat unpleasant results (you could look up Gen. 12:10–20). Famine was once more the driving force behind people moving from one land to another, which finds its echoes across the world today.

It seems that the Pharaoh of the day was genuinely pleased that Joseph's relatives were coming down into Egypt, but it is also a slightly amusing aside that Joseph feels he needs to school his brothers in what they must say before Pharaoh. The fact that he only picked out five of them may speak volumes about their lack of social graces!

To say that Jacob and family settled in the 'best' land must be seen as settling in the better part of that area in the Nile Delta. If the Egyptians were not living there themselves, that indicates it was only suitable for shepherds.

Through Joseph's forgiveness of his brothers all the family became reconciled and began a new life. This is a powerful analogy for the Christian for there is a very fine dividing line between reconciliation and redemption.

Discussion Starters

1. Put yourself in Joseph's shoes and say how you would have reacted to meeting the brothers after so many years.

2. Researching family trees is a popular hobby today, but imagine the reactions of Joseph's sons, Manasseh and Ephraim, on encountering such a large body of relatives with different language, dress and customs.

3. When Joseph sends his brothers back to fetch Jacob, he says to them 'Don't quarrel on the way!' What do you think lies behind that remark?

4. There is absolutely no mention in this section of Jacob's reaction when he realises that his sons so cruelly deceived him. Do we infer from this that Jacob forgave them? What are your thoughts on this?

5. Genesis 46:30 has been called an Old Testament *Nunc Dimittis*. What happening, personal or perhaps

international, would you like to experience before you die?

6. In Matthew's account of the Lord's Supper, he includes Jesus' words: 'This is my blood of the covenant, which is poured out for many for the forgiveness of sins' (Matt. 26:28). Discuss the place of Holy Communion in our own need of forgiveness.

7. Has your experience been that reconciliation automatically follows forgiveness? Discuss.

8. In what ways can the 'lesser person' – or country – be blessed by 'the greater' Person – or country (Heb. 7:7)?

9. Allow each other a few moments to silently reflect on the need for forgiveness and reconciliation in your own families.

Personal Application

Sadly, there are many churches and families which are torn apart because people will not forgive each other. The Bible reminds us that our Lord Jesus not only taught about forgiveness, but from the cross, in agony, He said: 'Father, forgive them' (Luke 23:34). None of us is perfect, we have all hurt people and stand in need of forgiveness, and as Christians we have an obligation to forgive and *move on*. It is not an optional extra. As Paul wrote, because God reconciled us to Himself through Jesus Christ, He has given to us the ministry of reconciliation (2 Cor. 5:18). What an overwhelming challenge to each one of us – what an effect it should have on our relationships and way of life – to minister forgiveness as we have been forgiven by our Father God.

Seeing Jesus in the Scriptures

In Joseph's astonishingly forgiving attitude and his heartfelt desire for reconciliation with his family, we see the mirror image of Jesus forgiving even those who crucified Him. His whole purpose was to reconcile sinful humanity to His loving Father, so that 'the kingdom of heaven' may be known on earth. The Joseph story suddenly illuminates that great verse from John 3:16. These are the words of Jesus Christ, and in His words we have the promise of forgiveness and reconciliation both in human terms and with our Creator God. The lives recorded in the Old Testament draw us to see God's intimate presence with His people and give greater understanding to the teaching of His Son, Jesus.

WEEK 7

Conclusion

Opening Icebreaker

Give each person in the group a piece of paper with the name of character from the chapters in Genesis studied so far. Ask each person to say what they think their character would remember about Joseph and why, eg Potiphar's wife, the butler, Benjamin, Asenath and so on ...

Bible Readings

- Genesis 47:13–49:12, 49:29–50:26
- 2 Corinthians 4:16–18
- Hebrews 11:21–22

Opening Our Eyes

This session might have appeared something of an anti-climax to the main thrust of Joseph's story, but in fact it lays the foundations for the beginning of the people of Israel as they increase to become a nation.

The whole of Genesis 48 and most of 49 are taken up with the instructions and blessings of the now-blind Jacob, impressing upon his family the importance of the covenant promises which one day would take them back to Canaan. The importance of the covenant cannot be overestimated as it retains a vital role in the contemporary situation between Israel and Palestine.

In the blessing Jacob gives to Manasseh and Ephraim we trace a sophisticated theological structure; Jacob acknowledges more than one aspect of Almighty God's being. First he speaks of God as being the God of his fathers, the God of the past, then as God of the present, his own shepherd in life, and also includes the work of the protecting Angel as being all part of the same God (48:15–16). Here is the ancient realisation of the awesome complexity of the Creator God and belief in God's involvement with both the individual and 'the people'.

Once again we read of a younger son receiving a greater blessing than the first-born. Jacob may have been blind and near death, but he deliberately put his right hand upon Ephraim, the younger boy. Several times in the Bible the Lord's purpose bypasses the great and powerful, whether that be individuals or nations. (Compare Micah 5:2 and Judges 6:15.)

The poetic format of Jacob's blessing upon his sons gives rise to the thought that probably his words were memorised and written relatively soon. Whether it received certain editorial additions in after years or not, it retains a paternal, no-frills appraisal of his sons' characters and fortunes.

We should just mention Reuben and Judah, as they were the two named brothers with ideas as to how to get rid of Joseph. Jacob's pain and disappointment in Reuben his first-born is obvious, referring to the episode with Bilhah. The prominent place is therefore given to the fearless Judah for whom Jacob foresees great things. This is the root of thought which will be met at various points through the rest of the Old Testament and finds its culmination in the birth of Jesus, in Bethlehem in the land of Judah.

Because of his promise to take his father's body for burial in Canaan, Joseph employs the costly and intricate Egyptian art of embalming. At the probable date of this story, embalming would have taken about 70 days; later the techniques speeded up to around a month.

Now that Jacob is dead, the brothers squirm in their guilt all over again. But Joseph brings the story to conclusion with a unique display of forgiveness; perhaps the key verse in the whole story is Genesis 50:20. Joseph forgave because he believed only God can put things right and God's requirement of His people is that they do not repay evil with evil. This is the golden link between the Old and the New Testaments as we receive teaching on forgiveness from Jesus Himself.

So Joseph ends his life a proud great-great-grandfather. In Egyptian culture 110 years symbolises the ideal age of a great man. He too was embalmed, leaving his body in an Egyptian coffin awaiting a time when he would be taken out of Egypt to the promised land of Canaan.

'And Joseph's bones, which the Israelites had brought up from Egypt, were buried at Shechem ...' (Josh. 24:32). Finally, Joseph had come home.

Discussion Starters

1. How did the brothers react to the death of their father?

2. Why do you think the Egyptians honoured Jacob with public mourning?

3. Contrast the splendid, funeral procession taking Jacob back to the burial ground of his ancestors, to the journey Jacob made in the first place, entering almost as a refugee, unseen, unknown.

4. What positive influence did Jacob have on Joseph?

5. What aspects of Joseph's life and character stand out and will be remembered by you?

6. With which character in the story do you sympathise?

7. Where would you imagine Joseph's Egyptian coffin was kept during the subsequent centuries of slavery, before Moses was able to take it with the Israelites at the time of the Exodus?

8. Have any of you been to the British Museum to see an Egyptian coffin? Can you describe it?

9. How do you think the children of Israel kept their faith and hope alive during their years of slavery?

Personal Application

Whatever happened in Joseph's life, he personified loyalty, integrity and faith. Considering the depths to which he was thrown, he comes across as an extraordinary man without malice; an outstanding role model in the annals of Jewish history. When we look back on our own lives and setbacks over which we have been powerless, if we are honest, we find whole layers of resentment and self-pity. We would do well to take an in-depth view of Joseph's response to events and be inspired by his unshakeable faith that God is the power beyond all human power. Joseph was faithful in small things and great things. Examine yourself and pray that your life can be seen as faithful as Joseph's.

Seeing Jesus in the Scriptures

Christians are quite familiar with the Messianic prophecies in the Old Testament, especially Isaiah and Micah, but it is exciting to glimpse the birth of these longings within Jacob's blessing on Judah. This is a dream for the future when paradise will be restored. The line of Judah will be the channel for this restoration in a perfected life. Matthew records the genealogy of Jesus, beginning with Abraham, naming Judah and David in the prestigious list of names. So Jesus is seen in a direct line from the patriarchs, and echoes the longing for the perfect life when He offered 'life in all its fulness'.

Above all, Jesus embodies all the virtues of Joseph and more – He is our perfect role model, the same yesterday, today and for ever.

Leader's Notes

Week 1: Teenager with Attitude

Opening Icebreaker

Sometimes groups do not know each other well and it can save embarrassment if name labels are worn for a couple of weeks. It just relaxes people to have a laugh about wearing colours to suit them and some people are acutely colour conscious. It will underline how different our tastes are!

Bible Readings

For this session it is necessary to read the entire chapter 37. If you can get hold of *The Dramatised Bible* you could use various members of the group to great effect. This adds interest, with different voices and so on, and makes people feel involved. The Leviticus verses deal with slave price, 1 Samuel with how David was sent to his brothers for news and Luke mentions Judas planning to 'sell' Jesus.

Aim of the Session

To see how Scripture uses 'story' in revealing the darker side of human nature. It is a lesson in attitudes and how hot-headed response to a situation can quickly get out of hand. Joseph's typically self-centred teenage attitude was enhanced by his father's indulgence. This session can look at family relationships in today's society where it is increasingly common for children to live with stepbrothers and sisters and for parents to compensate children with material things. Be especially sensitive to any deep pain or emotions that may be expressed. It may be appropriate to have a time of silence followed by a short prayer in which you offer painful memories to the heart of God.

With brilliant characterisation, this biography is a compelling tale overlaid with theological and moral implications. Everything in the Bible was written with a purpose and there is much for us to learn from Joseph. Jacob was a God-fearing man and yet his family was divided. Draw out the undercurrents from Joseph's informing on his half-brothers and encourage the group members to express their feelings from family hurts. The brothers' hatred could easily have led to murder and was only deferred by Judah's suggestion to sell the boy. Look at the story in Genesis 4:8 where jealousy leads to murder. Register the effect on Jacob when he thought his favourite son had been killed by wild animals. Jacob who had been so confident and slippery in his younger days had been dealt the most bitter of blows and seemed destined to go to his grave a broken man.

An often overlooked aspect of this story is the close relationship between father and son. We can assume that Joseph was taught to believe in the Lord God at his father's knee and surely this highlights the importance of being open and natural in talking with children about God. Note that Joseph would have received no further 'religious instruction' on the faith of his father and great-grandfather after the age of 17.

This is also a story about how God chooses individuals for His purpose and divine plan. From subsequent chapters, we see that Joseph had strong faith and moral standards. Does this underline how important it is to be diligent in teaching children to trust in God and live according to decent moral codes so that in their adult years they have a foundation of faith to meet with all life's complexities, sorrows and disappointments?

For the past 40 years or so, Old Testament stories have been sadly neglected and most people just think of Joseph as the boy with the multi-coloured coat. By the end of this session there should be sufficient meat on the bones of the story that the group grows to view Joseph and the whole family as real people, struggling with nomadic life in Canaan in second millennium BC.

Week 2: Sold into Egypt

Opening Icebreaker

Asking people who or what they have left at home opens up a greater understanding within the group. Some might have left an elderly parent and will need to dash off as soon as the session is over. Others may have left a pile of marking, a cat, children in the care of husband/wife and so on. This is invaluable in building trust which then leads later to open and interesting discussions.

Bible Readings

Genesis 39. Again, it is necessary to read the whole chapter to get the overall picture. You could ask the group to scan the chapter the previous week as there's a lot to it. It reads easily.

Psalm 139 is the cry that wherever we are, God is there with us. He knows and understands. Hebrews encourages Christians to hold fast to their beliefs just as poor old Joseph clung to his faith.

Aim of the Session

Bring out the dramatic change in Joseph's fortunes. One day he was the pampered favourite, telling tales on his brothers, avoiding getting his hands dirty, lavished with all good things and the next he was shackled and tramping off with strangers to be sold in a foreign country. Language, customs, food – all components of the culture shock. Then, when things were looking good and Joseph was in charge of Potiphar's household, once more his life disintegrated. He became a prisoner which was even worse than a slave. Cruel twists at an impressionable stage of life.

Explore together Joseph's reactions to his fate. His attitude seems grounded in the faith his father taught him and which, though he was far from home and family, was to mould and sustain him throughout his life. The Lord was with him as much in the pit as when he was swaggering about in his multi-coloured coat. The Lord was with him in Potiphar's luxurious house and also in the squalid prison. Compare Psalm 139:7–12. Encourage the group to acknowledge the Lord's presence in their own good and dark times too.

This episode highlights the age-old theme of sexual immorality and the consequences. Sometimes we are so intrigued by gossip about celebrities, or just take for granted things 'happen', that it is easy to overlook the consequences of lustful gratification. When temptation comes along, two people may think they are the only ones involved but sadly the ripples of infidelity spread wide. Potiphar 'burned with anger'. In those few words lie all the broken trust and hurt from which some people never recover.

Joseph shows strength of character and loyalty to his master. In this strongest and most personal of temptations, Joseph conducts himself impeccably and a man who can be reliable in such a situation will surely be responsible in every other aspect of life.

Don't let the group forget that Jacob is still grieving. He is inconsolable but the brothers keep up the deceit that Joseph is dead.

Week 3: Dreams

Opening Icebreaker

The group should be getting to know each other by now and feeling comfortable to share. Dreams can be alarming or funny and humour always brightens a session. We all have dream occupations and, if there are too many people to speak in the time allotted, it could easily be carried over into the next week. Try to make sure that nobody feels squeezed out and also insist on brevity – you may have a psychoanalyst in your midst!

Bible Readings

You will be looking at six dreams in this session, Joseph's two, those of the cup-bearer and the baker and Pharaoh's two dreams. Different voices for each character's dream would be a good idea. Also note the tone of the Deuteronomy reading, written at a much later period and showing the distaste for other cultures. It may be possible within your time to express the difference between a dream whilst unconscious and a conscious dream towards which people can work for the good of the society.

Aim of the Session

Much of the Wisdom literature in the Scriptures is coloured by the ancient culture of Egypt. The continuing tension of syncretism faced by various tribal groups living and moving around the biblical lands is perhaps best encapsulated in Ecclesiastes 5:7: 'Much dreaming and many words are meaningless. Therefore stand in awe of God.' This sets our stage.

Joseph has been 'forcibly carried off from the land of the Hebrews' (Gen. 40:15) and flung into a nation and a class structure vastly different from his own. This was to be an amazing learning curve for the young man and an experience which brought out the best in his character. In the prison he learned to listen – both to his companions and to his God, and this is one of our most serious failings of today.

It's humbling to consider Joseph's life at this point. He is at rock-bottom with no glimmer of rescue, yet he had not become eaten up with bitterness and resentment. Nowhere in the narrative does it mention that Joseph prayed, but his whole demeanour implies a life-saving relationship with his father's God. Even in prison, he was trustworthy and pleasant and concerned with the welfare of others. He does not come across as ingratiating but as patient and reliable at all times.

Explain to the group the influential role of chief cup-bearer and chief baker; they were crucial to the Pharaoh's health and well-being. The baker's baskets were probably wickerwork and let's not forget his professional expertise with all those varieties to tempt his master. Joseph had to learn the hard lesson that people are fickle and unreliable and it must have been the severest test of his patience and faith to realise that his 'favour' had been forgotten.

Two years later, Pharaoh is really stressed by his dreams which are like hallucinatory nightmares. The fact that he was prepared to listen to a Hebrew slave/prisoner, the lowest of the low, could be evidence that he was one of the non-Egyptian 'Hyksos' kings of around 1700 BC, or he may just have been plain desperate! When Joseph interprets for him – it seems to be such an obvious explanation – the court magicians must have been furious.

Week 4: A Man of Distinction

Opening Icebreaker

It is easy to overlook the quantity of religious beliefs and figureheads that have been worshipped by various cultures and it will be an eye-opener to list just how many 'gods' are taking peoples' attention today. The Semitic nomads in the land of Canaan knew that they were in a vulnerable minority – it's somewhat uncomfortable to realise that Christians are a vulnerable minority in most countries in this twenty-first century.

Bible Readings

The central reading from Genesis 41 continues our saga. Psalm 105 shows us how the Psalms were used as the folk songs of the people containing their history as much as their worship. The Philippians reading underlines that in the power of the Holy Spirit we all have the strength to move on.

Aim of the Session

Perhaps the most important theme to draw from this session is that God knows and understands and enables those who believe in Him to come through the most bleak experiences. We, in our turn, have to show and nurture integrity, justice and compassion and when people live like that – lives change for the good of all.

In the ancient world there was an undisputed link between clan or tribe and its deity. The god was elevated to the head of the 'house', and in this story we find that Joseph continues to live in a covenant relationship in foreign surroundings and is seen by everyone as a man of outstanding maturity and wisdom. Here is the power of witness to our faith.

It might be helpful to have a map of the Nile Delta showing all the tributaries in comparison to the land of Canaan. We are conditioned to watch the weather forecast after every news bulletin even though the weather rarely affects or disrupts our daily routine. The weather for biblical people was a life and death battle. Rain, and therefore a water supply, ensured life. Drought brought the stark sceptre of death.

Also, consider the trading world. Looking at a map, it is incredible how the trading routes criss-crossed cultures carrying goods, fashions, equipment, remedies, stories, ideas and just the general pulse of human activity. Egypt was a cultivated, proud and ancient civilisation, the hub of learning for maths, science and engineering – think of the pyramids! Horses and chariots are likely to have been imported from Greece or even as far north as Russia. Draw attention to the use of ceremonial robes and chain of office, which is something we still do today and which traditional costumes, such as Yeomen of the Guard, Lord Mayors of London, Garter Knights, tourists flock to see.

Joseph needed to be a man of iron resolve to make sure corruption did not get a hold on the granaries at the distribution points. We witness on our television screens the difficulties of fair dispersal of aid and this was a huge logistical operation which had to last for seven years. Joseph was God's man in the right place at the right time.

Week 5: Corn in Egypt

Opening Icebreaker

Only people living in the most rural areas will need to store essential items as part of their way of life. For most of us our food is readily accessible. To get the group to pin-point what *is* essential helps to raise an awareness of our own blessings and the daily struggles for too many of our brothers and sisters across our world. Hopefully, it will be challenging to imagine sharing when we ourselves are in need.

Bible Readings

Yes, this is a mega-chunk to get through but this is a Bible study and there is no other way round it but to read the story as recorded.

Aim of the Session

As we read these verses it is almost like watching a video, so vividly does the writer portray the action and cast. Help the group to catch the overall picture in Canaan of increasing desperation as food dwindles. Jacob's family is large, he is old, but it appears that the brothers, who are also responsible for families, are dragging their heels with regards to finding food elsewhere. The reports of food in Egypt come via the traders and nomads and probably those who have already been down to collect grain.

The mention of donkeys and the gifts of balm, honey, myrrh, almonds and pistachio nuts again help the biblical tale to come alive. There are such human touches, in that Jacob comes across as a gruff, intransigent old man, paralysed by fear of losing Benjamin, yet it is he who orders his other sons to get themselves down into Egypt to bring back grain.

Point out that from this account Joseph is very much a hands-on viceroy. Pharaoh had said: 'Go to Joseph and do what he tells you' (41:55), so we may assume that he routinely visited the aid centres making sure all was fair and things were running smoothly. It may also mean that Joseph was taking a particular interest in the grain distribution for the people coming down from the Canaan area, hoping and praying that someone from his own family might appear. Dressed in his fine Egyptian robes, the brothers would never have suspected his identity and so when they are busy talking away in Hebrew, they are totally unaware that Joseph was following every word.

Joseph must have felt the hairs on the back of his head tingle as his brothers bowed before him and he remembered his boyhood dream. Surely, this was God's providence and mercy extended to Abraham's progeny. You could make the observation that by Joseph's astute economic programme, he became the first saviour of his people.

It is interesting to note three names used for God in this passage: Elohim, Shaddai and Yahweh, each bringing out different aspects of His attributes and the making of a people in covenant with Him.

Remember that the story of Joseph is not merely an intriguing family saga from way back in the mists of time, but a way of showing how God holds together a disintegrated family and out of alienation and famine brings reunion and life. Sometimes we have to be reminded that this is our God too.

Personal Application

All families are so incredibly different. Yet most have to cope with tensions of one sort or another. Sometimes there is irretrievable breakdown in relationships, broken trust and a great deal of hurt and guilt to which no one ever likes to admit. Joseph shows grace and mercy in admirable measure. There may be situations all too close to home which have festered in our lives over a long period, and God is nudging us to such a magnanimous spirit of grace and mercy. People do change with the years – and that includes ourselves.

Seeing Jesus in the Scriptures

The great theme of sacrificial love will recur in Isaiah's concept of the 'suffering servant' and find its culmination in the sacrifice of our Lord Jesus Christ. Joseph had trusted in his God to deliver him and Jacob trusted in his God to deliver his family and so fulfil the covenant given to Abraham. Jesus trusted in His Father and said about His death: 'This cup is the new covenant in my blood ...' (1 Cor. 11:25).

The relationship of trust had been broken time and time again by the people but God's nature is faithful and merciful. As the Israelite nation proved unreliable to their God, so the disciples, at the ultimate test, proved unreliable and ran away (Mark 14:50).

Week 6: Forgiveness and Reconciliation

Opening Icebreaker

The purpose of this icebreaker is to get the group thinking about the enormous upheaval involved in moving house, jobs, schools, pets, livestock et al and, together with *all* their relatives begin somewhere new. There are bound to be families with members who would refuse point blank to move! An aged Granny or a daughter who is 'in love' etc. Logistics are problem enough in the twenty-first century so be sympathetic to Jacob and co.

Bible Readings

There is an immense amount of detail in this session. On a completely historical note, it shows the huge journeys undertaken and the generally easy movement of the semi-nomadic tribes around the Fertile Crescent, down into Egypt and beyond. If you use a map, look at the difference in the route taken by the brothers down into Egypt and the detour which Jacob made to visit Beersheba to pray at his father's grave before leaving Canaan. The New Testament references tell us of one of the main themes of the Bible – forgiveness and reconciliation – and the response expected from Christians.

Aim of the Session

This session is the nub of the whole story: forgiveness and reconciliation in human terms is but a reflection of divine forgiveness and redemption. God brings blessing out of situations, irrespective of human intentions, wilfulness and sin. Explain to the group that it was through stories and parables that people learnt the nature of their God and the uncomfortable truth that God expected a change in their attitudes and way of life. After all, it's far easier to see where *other* people are going wrong than where we ourselves are behaving badly. But, as the old saying goes: It's the truth that hurts!

Even if we don't have a family ourselves, we can imagine the 'behind-the-scenes' squirming, arguments and excuses that would have characterised the brothers' immediate reaction in discovering the boy they sold was now the second most powerful man in Egypt. Recall for the group that Joseph declares four times his belief that it was God who sent him to Egypt, and that he was there for the specific purpose of saving the lives of his own family as well as his adopted country.

People often sing the well-loved chorus: 'Freely, freely …' but let's pause to look at the first verse:

> God forgave my sin in Jesus' name,
> I've been born again in Jesus' name
> And in Jesus' name I come to you
> To share His love as He told me to.

Surely, this is the gospel of forgiveness and reconciliation in modern terms. Draw out the message that the Bible is not just for other people, it is God's Word directly to us in our own unique setting. Only by recognising and responding to God's forgiveness can we begin to forgive ourselves and each other. The vividly sketched characters of Jacob and his family enable us to see that their experience mirrors basic human experience and God's constant, guiding hand of compassion. If there is time, share the words from 1 John 1:8–9: 'If we claim to be without sin, we deceive ourselves … If we confess our sins, he is faithful and just and will forgive us our sins ...'

Encourage the group to see that there is so much more to what is *not* recorded. It is a living story, passed down through the generations to be a help, comfort and example to those who put their faith in the God of Abraham, Isaac and Israel.

You could close by saying the Lord's Prayer together.

Week 7: Conclusion

Opening Icebreaker

This gives a chance for a mixture of light-hearted and serious observations. Sometimes there are some extremely serious points hidden behind flippancy. It also recaps on the story's large and varied cast list.

Bible Readings
Time may not allow for reading the verses concerning the final five years of the famine. This is not so important, nor are the blessings for all the sons. The New Testament verses fit neatly as reference texts and underline the importance of Joseph to the early Christians.

Aim of the Session
It is important for the leader to put across the concept of covenant. Firstly, in the mind of the patriarchs, secondly in the national consciousness which sustained the Israelites through their horrendous history. Thirdly, how Jews relate to the idea of the covenant today.

The covenant made between God and Abraham was preserved and taken into Egypt like some priceless family heirloom, and over the years it gradually turned from a precious promise at the centre of their faith, into an obsession. This is why Joseph's role in enabling his family to come through the years of famine and flourish in a new country was crucial to the continuation of the covenant. On his deathbed, Joseph reiterated the covenant promise (50:24). The essential format was that God had promised and God would be faithful, therefore everything was seen by the writers of Scripture as pertaining to God's will, purpose and providence.

Another remarkable aspect within these closing chapters is the way in which Jacob speaks about God. Not just as God, but as caring Shepherd and guardian Angel. The way is paved for the multifaceted concept of the One Living God being Rock, Redeemer, Shepherd, King, Saviour, Father, Immanuel, yesterday, today and for ever.

The narrative flow is lost in these last chapters and, at times, it can appear as a somewhat disjointed read. However, there are some poignant gems which add vital colour and symbolism to this fascinating saga. Genesis

47:27 has a direct link with God's words in Genesis 1 'be fruitful and multiply'.

In such a hot and dusty region, blindness was by no means uncommon, and by reading this story of Joseph we realise that Jacob goes blind in old age just as his father Isaac had done.

You may like to draw attention to the phrase 'gathered to my people' (49:29). No generation has been comfortable in describing 'death' but in Jacob's words there is a hint that he is not afraid to die, and death is seen as a natural return to one's roots, rather than a finite end.

The brothers' reaction to their father's death shows that they just couldn't believe Joseph could genuinely forgive them. As with all guilty people, they had a string of excuses and explanations and ways of being inventive with the truth.

Perhaps the key verse to the entire story is 50:20. Here Joseph declares his life-long faith in God. Whatever evil his brothers had plotted, God had other ideas. Joseph was not brushing aside their malevolence but asserting that God's power was supreme. Joseph was no longer a dreamer but a realist of huge experience through which he had learnt humility and trust. As we progress in our walk with the Lord, we too will need to face the sometimes brutal reality of peoples' actions, but we can face these experiences with God's strength.

Don't let the group get hung up over the incredible ages recorded here. The dating system was not the same as ours. What is undeniably true is that Jacob and Joseph lived to be very old men. It's interesting to note that Joshua also lived to 110.

The leader's task will have been well done if the sessions

enabled the group to see in this story real people battling with real issues. We too have our own battles. But nothing we face is ever outside the sphere of God's love and forgiveness and in the power of His Holy Spirit the ministry of reconciliation is our response to His covenant promise.

National Distributors

UK: (and countries not listed below)
CWR, Waverley Abbey House, Waverley Lane, Farnham, Surrey GU9 8EP.
Tel: (01252) 784700 Outside UK (44) 1252 784700

AUSTRALIA: CMC Australasia, PO Box 519, Belmont, Victoria 3216.
Tel: (03) 5241 3288 Fax: (03) 5241 3290

CANADA: Cook Communications Ministries, PO Box 98, 55 Woodslee Avenue, Paris, Ontario N3L 3E5.
Tel: 1800 263 2664

GHANA: Challenge Enterprises of Ghana, PO Box 5723, Accra.
Tel: (021) 222437/223249 Fax: (021) 226227

HONG KONG: Cross Communications Ltd, 1/F, 562A Nathan Road, Kowloon.
Tel: 2780 1188 Fax: 2770 6229

INDIA: Crystal Communications, 10-3-18/4/1, East Marredpalli, Secunderabad – 500026, Andhra Pradesh.
Tel/Fax: (040) 27737145

KENYA: Keswick Books and Gifts Ltd, PO Box 10242, Nairobi. Tel: (02) 331692/226047
Fax: (02) 728557

MALAYSIA: Salvation Book Centre (M) Sdn Bhd, 23 Jalan SS 2/64, 47300 Petaling Jaya, Selangor.
Tel: (03) 78766411/78766797 Fax: (03) 78757066/78756360

NEW ZEALAND: CMC Australasia, PO Box 303298, North Harbour, Auckland 0751.
Tel: 0800 449 408 Fax: 0800 449 049

NIGERIA: FBFM, Helen Baugh House, 96 St Finbarr's College Road, Akoka, Lagos.
Tel: (01) 7747429/4700218/825775/827264

PHILIPPINES: OMF Literature Inc, 776 Boni Avenue, Mandaluyong City.
Tel: (02) 531 2183 Fax: (02) 531 1960

SINGAPORE: Alby Commercial Enterprises Pte Ltd, 95 Kallang Avenue #04-00, AIS Industrial Building, 339420. Tel: (65) 629 27238 Fax: (65) 629 27235

SOUTH AFRICA: Struik Christian Books, 80 MacKenzie Street, PO Box 1144, Cape Town 8000.
Tel: (021) 462 4360 Fax: (021) 461 3612

SRI LANKA: Christombu Publications (Pvt) Ltd, Bartleet House, 65 Braybrooke Place, Colombo 2.
Tel: (9411) 2421073/2447665

TANZANIA: CLC Christian Book Centre, PO Box 1384, Mkwepu Street, Dar es Salaam.
Tel/Fax: (022) 2119439

USA: Cook Communications Ministries, PO Box 98, 55 Woodslee Avenue, Paris, Ontario N3L 3E5, Canada.
Tel: 1800 263 2664

ZIMBABWE: Word of Life Books (Pvt) Ltd, Christian Media Centre, 8 Aberdeen Road, Avondale, PO Box A480 Avondale, Harare. Tel: (04) 333355 or 091301188

For email addresses, visit the CWR website: www.cwr.org.uk

CWR is a Registered Charity – Number 294387

CWR is a Limited Company registered in England – Registration Number 1990308

Cover to Cover Complete

This takes you on a chronological journey through the Bible, allowing you to follow the events as they happened - and enabling you to see more clearly the unfolding of God's purpose over the centuries. It's also constructed to encourage you to read the entire Bible text in one year.

Far more than just the text alone, this Bible comes complete with maps, charts, illustrations, diagrams, a timeline and much more: everything you need to enhance your understanding as you read. It uses the highly-respected Holman Christian Standard Bible (HCSB) text. There is also an accompanying section on our website, giving access to even more information about key people and events, weekly discussion questions for group study, and much more.

Format: Hardback

ISBN: 978-1-85345-433-2

£19.99

Also available in the bestselling *Cover to Cover Bible Study* series

1 Corinthians
Growing a Spirit-filled church
ISBN: 978-1-85345-374-8

1 Timothy
Healthy churches – effective Christians
ISBN: 978-1-85345-291-8

2 Timothy and Titus
Vital Christianity
ISBN: 978-1-85345-338-0

23rd Psalm
The Lord is my Shepherd
ISBN: 978-1-85345-449-3

Colossians
In Christ alone
ISBN: 978-1-85345-405-9

Ecclesiastes
Hard questions and spiritual answers
ISBN: 978-1-85345-371-7

Ephesians
Claiming your inheritance
ISBN: 978-1-85345-229-1

Fruit of the Spirit
Growing more like Jesus
ISBN: 978-1-85345-375-5

Genesis 1–11
Foundations of reality
ISBN: 978-1-85345-404-2

God's Rescue Plan
Finding God's fingerprints on human history
ISBN: 978-1-85345-294-9

Great Prayers of the Bible
Applying them to our lives today
ISBN: 978-1-85345-253-6

Hebrews
Jesus – simply the best
ISBN: 978-1-85345-337-3

Hosea
The love that never fails
ISBN: 978-1-85345-290-1

James
Faith in action
ISBN: 978-1-85345-293-2

Jeremiah
The passionate prophet
ISBN: 978-1-85345-372-4

John's Gospel
Exploring the seven miraculous signs
ISBN: 978-1-85345-295-6

Joseph
The power of forgiveness and reconciliation
ISBN: 978-1-85345-252-9

Mark
Life as it is meant to be lived
ISBN: 978-1-85345-233-8

Moses
Face to face with God
ISBN: 978-1-85345-336-6

Nehemiah
Principles for life
ISBN: 978-1-85345-335-9

Parables
Communicating God on earth
ISBN: 978-1-85345-340-3

Philemon
From slavery to freedom
ISBN: 978-1-85345-453-0

Philippians
Living for the sake of the gospel
ISBN: 978-1-85345-421-9

Proverbs
Living a life of wisdom
ISBN: 978-1-85345-373-1

Revelation 4–22
The Lamb wins! Christ's final victory
ISBN: 978-1-85345-411-0

Rivers of Justice
Responding to God's call to righteousness today
ISBN: 978-1-85345-339-7

Ruth
Loving kindness in action
ISBN: 978-1-85345-231-4

The Covenants
God's promises and their relevance today
ISBN: 978-1-85345-255-0

The Divine Blueprint
God's extraordinary power in ordinary lives
ISBN: 978-1-85345-292-5

The Holy Spirit
Understanding and experiencing Him
ISBN: 978-1-85345-254-3

The Image of God
His attributes and character
ISBN: 978-1-85345-228-4

The Letter to the Romans
Good news for everyone
ISBN: 978-1-85345-250-5

The Prodigal Son
Amazing grace
ISBN: 978-1-85345-412-7

The Second Coming
Living in the light of Jesus' return
ISBN: 978-1-85345-422-6

The Sermon on the Mount
Life within the new covenant
ISBN: 978-1-85345-370-0

The Tabernacle
Entering into God's presence
ISBN: 978-1-85345-230-7

The Uniqueness of our Faith
What makes Christianity distinctive?
ISBN: 978-1-85345-232-1

£3.99 each (plus p&p)

Price correct at time of printing

Cover to Cover Every Day

Cover to Cover Every Day is a set of bimonthly daily reading notes that gives you an in-depth study of the Bible. Over a five-year period, you will be taken through each book of the Bible. Every issue includes contributions from two different authors, with a reflection on a psalm each weekend by Philip Greenslade.

- Short in-depth Bible study every day
- Rolling five-year curriculum covering every book of the Bible
- Bible references and a prayer for every day
- Contributions from well-known authors including R.T. Kendall, Philip Greenslade, Joel Edwards and Ian Coffey

Format: Booklet

ISSN: 1744-0114

Price: £2.25